WICCA ALTAR FOR BEGINNERS

THE COMPLETE GUIDE
How to Set Up and Take Care,
What to do and What NOT to do
+ 10 Spells

DAPHNE BROOKS

TABLE OF CONTENTS

WICCA ALTAR FOR BEGINNERS

INTRODUCTION

There are a lot of misconstrued interpretations about the Wicca altar. Contrary to what most people think, Wiccan altars are important in certain religious beliefs and it is wrong to come to a hasty conclusion about religious ethnic you have no understanding of.

Wicca altar is an exalted place / structure of worship that is used by a Wiccan worshipper / practitioner. The practitioner uses the altar for various reasons that suit his/her needs. The practitioner may settle to use the altars for purposes of praying, chanting, or any other uses that fit their discretion. Upon the altar, the individual who makes use of the altar makes decisions regarding the suitable symbols or images to use. The items upon the altar are basically symbolic to the practitioner and are considered very essential.

Just like every altar symbolizes peace, the Wicca altar is very important in that creates an inner communion between the physical and spiritual element. Except you understand how it works, you may never really behold the beauty of the Wicca altar. Altars are necessary to establish a place of balance between the different elements of nature. It is considered as a sacred place of devotion. It is much easier to pour out your innermost thoughts, needs, and desires at the altar without the fear of being wrongly judged by other individuals.

One exceptional difference between the Wicca altar and other altars is that the Wicca altar creates room for a totality of unbiased expression and paves the way for individuals to express the longing of their souls and appreciate the wonders of spirituality. Every individual is a spiritual being and that is why a lot of times people attribute the existence of men to spiritual issues. The body of humans is considered a temple that is to be treated with a sense of utmost care and attention. The desire to protect the body and keep it away from unpleasant things also applies in the manner in which the Wicca altar should be treated. The human heart shields a temple. To path to the heart is a spiritual process. The reason is not far- fetched. The heart exists but is considered abstract in that it can't be seen except for certain circumstances.

Ironically, the fact that the heart is considered abstract doesn't take away its relevance to the human body functioning. This is likened to the Wicca altar. A lot of times there are arguments based on the relevance or existence of the spiritual powers of the Wiccan altar. Many times, people do not believe the spirituality of the Wicca altars or the presence of the gods and goddesses that protect their worshippers because they cannot see these gods with their eyes. The fact that they can't be seen doesn't take away the fact that they actually exist.

To make it easier, the Wiccan altar has a lot of symbols which create a deep sense of closeness between the people that worship at the altar and the true meaning of what the altar represents. It is easier to believe what you can see, hear or taste. So, the physical structure of the Wiccan altar brings a feeling of availability to the mind of its believers, and as such, they benefit tremendously from the magic that is available on the altar.

It is undeniably true that a lot of people have separate altars without even realizing it. Your personal altar could be a collection of pictures that reminds you of home or loved ones or a portrait of your favorite pet. Why? This is so because individuals crave an image that symbolizes what they need. For the spiritual part, the Wicca altar helps in creating a sense of connection between what the heart desires and the means to actually achieving all that is conceived in the heart. It is a lot easier to get various collections or images of what you believe in and put it on an altar. The essence of this is to put up symbols and images that uplift the totality of your being. In this way, the altar becomes an important part of your life.

The purpose of those chosen symbols or images is to remind you of your existence and purpose in life. As a matter of fact, everyone that breathes air has a purpose in life and until that purpose is achieved life doesn't seem fulfilling.

The Wicca uplifts your soul and creates a connection between your spirituality and physical existence. The beauty of this altar is embedded in the reality that there are no rules to where it is structured. It can be put up virtually everywhere and anywhere. One key thing to understand is that wherever the Wiccan altar is set up, it becomes a home for the gods and goddesses that govern such an altar. Hence, it is important to choose a suitable place to set up the Wiccan altar.

There are only one means of staying connected to divinity. This is through the Wicca altar. The altar provides a sustainable relationship between you and the spiritual being. The only evidence and reminder of the relationship you have with the spiritual being is the presence of the altar. This altar must be regarded with reverence and absolute care. A lot of things that go on in your life whether good or bad are attributed to the Wicca altar. The way and manner you treat the Wiccan altar reveal how things work for you. If the situations in your life are not working as planned, then chances are that you have failed to do right by the altar. So, it is essential to consider your attitude towards the altar.

The powers upon the altar work magic provided you understand how to treat the altar. If at some point in time you feel that there are loopholes in your life that need to be attended to, then there is a need to go back to the altar and put it in its appropriate condition.

It is often said that Life has some rules that govern it. This is not entirely true in the case of the Wicca altar. There are no rules to setting up your Wicca altar or a suitable way to worship at the altar. The way one individual treats his Wicca altar is totally different from the way another does. At the end of the day, it works for both parties perfectly irrespective of the fact that they didn't use the same pattern for their altars.

Never be carried away by the incessant ideas of others when it concerns the state or beauty of your altars. One sacrosanct thing to take cognizant of is that the Wicca altar is beautiful in different ways. So, never stop respecting the beauty of your Wicca altar. Appreciate, respect and love the altar and watch it do wonders for you.

In the course of this book, a lot of informative details will be revealed. The intent of this book is to uncover the too many mysteries surrounding the Wicca altar and also reveal the beauty of the altar as well as how to treat the Wicca altar like one who fully understands the beauty and magic concealed in the altar. Hence, it is important to state that this book is not entirely a beginner's guide but a complete detailed book that can teach beginners all they need to know about the Wicca altar. More so, intermediate users rest assured that this book has them covered as it adequately discusses a lot of issues, answers a lot of questions and dispels the too many doubts contained in the heart of many. This is the ideal book for all who hope to get it right!

A LITTLE BIT OF HISTORY

Wiccan is a religious practice that sprung up in the 1950s. the birth of Wicca began with Gardner and a few others who claimed to believe in the Wicca faith. According to this sect, they had been introduced into the faith by their ancestors. So, to them, their traditional religion was Wicca and as such, they struggled to keep the faith growing by doing what was expected of them.

Sybil Leek, Charles Cardell amongst others were the few that claimed that the Wicca faith was their traditional form of prayers. Coincidentally, their form of belief was similar to that practiced by Gardner. As such, it didn't take a long time for people to accept their views and explanations.
Many individuals settled to accept that the form of religion those individuals practiced were solely Wicca but for others, it was termed a traditional form of witchcraft. So, the practice was accepted to a minimal point.

The name "Wicca" was introduced by Charles Cardell. He didn't want to refer to the religion as some sort of witchcraft. So, he settled to refer to it as either Wicca or Wicen. Thus the term "Wiccan" was used to refer to any witch-cult practice among the people. An attempt was made to reconcile all the witch – cult-based religions but the effort proved to be unrealistic and futile. After a few years Gardner introduced Wiccan, it spread its tentacles across various populations and countries. The religion had suddenly spread across different countries like Scotland and Ireland. However, in the early part of the 1960s, the religion spread across the different English countries like the united states and Australia.

The religion thrived in Australia and the individuals welcomed with him with open arms because of their pagan attitude and worship ways unlike in the United States. In the United States, the Wicca religion was introduced by an English man and his wife. The English man, Raymond Buckland, together with his wife, Rosemary who had just relocated to the USA had to accept the religion accepted the religion they were introduced into the faith in a ceremony in Britain. The couple went back to America and founded a coven where they were able to practice the Gardnerian religion by making use of the book of shadows. The coven was later managed by another couple and they referred to the book of shadows to initiate new members into the practice. This spurned to a lot of interest among the population of the United States and they decided to own their personal covens. This, in turn, helped to make the religion spread faster among the people of the United States as such it became easier to propagate the religion by the word of mouth rather than initiation.

Another form of religion was introduced in the United States in the 1960s and it was not in conformity with the Gardnerian practice. However, the first Wicca church became recognized in 1972. In 2000, the Wiccan practice also became popular with other countries like South Africa and India.

In the 1960s, a man emerged and claimed to be initiated into the witchcraft practice by his grandmother. The man was identified as Alex Sanders. After much research was carried out, it was proved that he had been initiated into the Gardnerian coven by his grandmother. The research also proved that his grandmother was experienced in crafting good crafts. His reputation also increased when he married Maxine Sanders. The couple referred to themselves as the king and queen of witches. The couple had some witches and covens and also expanded their coven. At some point in time, Sanders combined both the elements of Wicca and Christianity together and this didn't go down well with the rest of the coven members. Sanders explained such a combination by stating that the fusion of both religions would help to combat the elements of satanic manipulations.

When some members insulted his motive and intention for fusing both religious practices, Sanders called it bluff and stated that they were not being knowledgeable in their actions. In the year 1973, the marriage between Alex and Maxine was annulled as a result of Alex's bisexuality. Rather than a change from being a bisexual, Alex focused his attention on how to incorporate homosexual men into the religion. He sought to create ways the religion can accommodate homosexuals. At some point in time, he realized his follies ad apologized for his past mistakes. He also made attempts to create a fusion between Gardnerian and Sanders, but he later gave up the ghost in 1988.

The United States witnessed a lot of forms of Wiccan practices in 1970. The proponent of Wicca at this period tried to fuse the Gardnerian and Sanders practice of Wicca and this caused quite a stir among the believers who thought that it wasn't supposed to be so. Raymond Buckland who introduced the religion to the United States also left the practice and introduced another type of practice. The seax- Wiccan was introduced by Raymond so that any willing person could practice. He also made available its rites and rituals and documented it in a book.

Budapest came up with a form of Wiccan practice that encouraged the females to practice religion with fear or favor. This form of Wiccan was largely referred to as a feminist approach to Wiccan. This approach was made to embrace females into practicing the religion irrespective of their lineage. So, any willing female was at the right of practicing the religion without any restriction whatsoever. The Dianic approach to Seax was more to honor a goddess.

Wiccans are always expected to swear an oath of secrecy that would restrict them from discussing the activities of their rituals to anybody. The Gardnerian practice of Wiccan did not comply with this oath. Rather, they preferred to carry out their rituals in the full glare of the people without pretense. This went on for a while until there was some sort of misconception about the Wiccan practice. A lot of people started to attribute the practice to a lot of evil and darkness. So, to prevent these situations, the Wiccans decided to reveal its operations to the general public and avoid the unpleasant situation of attributing the practice to something evil.

Suddenly, Wiccan became more pronounced than it ever was. A lot of people got to know about the Wiccan religion and sought to become members of the cult. The entertainment was not left out as it made some movies that revolved around Wiccan religion and practices. One of the movies produced by the entertainment sector didn't reveal the real intent of the Wiccan religion and depicted a bad image of the religion. So, to curb these effects and unwanted imagery of the practice, the various Wiccan covens placed a strict restriction on the acceptance of members into their coven. The age limit for participation became eighteen years and above. This made it difficult for inquisitive teenagers to gain entry into the coven. As such, they turned to their books to seek answers to the questions that plagued their hearts. Of course, the books provided all the needed information to satisfy the curiosity of various

14

individuals.

A lot of teenagers are interested in religion because it addresses issues that a lot of other religions do not address adequately. This has caused an uproar among different practitioners who feel that teenagers are not expected to participate in the practice. To worsen the situation, a certain twelve –year- old teen was killed as a result of practicing the faith. The presence of the internet also worsened the situation and made Wicca get a large ground of popularity. As a matter of fact, Wiccan was regarded as a common witch- cult and didn't get enough recognition but today in virtually every major city, Wicca is greatly permissible. The Wiccan is not just any other cult, but it is now regarded as a religion. It has successfully integrated different parts and sects of people together. The interest of a lot of practitioners has successfully caused the religion to gain recognition. As a matter of fact, there was a case of a Wiccan wedding in the year 2004. The Wiccan wedding was performed in the United Kingdom.

TYPES OF WICCA ALTAR

There are quite a lot of Wicca altar types. Like I had earlier stated in the introductory part of this book, there are no rules to how your Wiccan altar looks like. The type of a Wiccan altar used depends on the various factors. These factors could either be based on family background, preferences, financial situation and societal beliefs.

In considering the type of Wicca altar to settle for, it is important to bear in mind that there are different situations that you must take cognizant of. First and foremost, are you comfortable with your faith? Do you want to make your faith known to everyone? Do you have enough space to accommodate the size of the altar you prefer? All of these factors must be duly considered before settling for a particular Wicca altar type. Irrespective of people's opinion, the choice of your Wicca altar must be solely dependent on the reason for your choice in the first place.

THE DIFFERENT TYPES OF WICCA ALTAR ARE:

The home-based altar:

Just like the name presupposes, this type of altars are found in Wiccan homes. The family may or may not share the same faith, but it doesn't make the altar less important. This altar type in most cases is placed in a strategic position of the house; thereby, exuding a sense of relevance and importance to the family. Such altars never lose its importance and may not become unimportant for a very long time. These altars may get different forms or even take a different shape according to different seasons and periods, but it will lose its place in the home.

The home-based altar type is not expected to become

too conspicuous for the fact that the family may entertain guests at different points in time. Some of the guests may not necessarily accept your choice of faith. So, it is important to avoid cases where the guests start feeling uncomfortable around the house because of the presence of the altar. This implies that the Wicca altar should not be too Wiccan based. More so, some family members may not totally accept the faith you share. In other to curb the occurrences of disagreement between the family members, it is necessary to be moderate in decorating the home-based Wiccan altar. Simple symbols and images should be used in the home-based altar style bearing in mind different militating factors.

The private Wiccan altar:

This altar type is solely for personal use. An individual can settle for this altar type especially when such a person is not ready to entertain contrary views to the faith they share. A lot of people will always come up with a lot of ideas on how to go about your religious beliefs. If you are a discreet person who appreciates the faith you share and wouldn't want anyone to dissuade you from going with your preferred faith, this is the best Wiccan altar type for you to settle for.

This altar type can be set up in the comfort of your homes or closets. In this way, nobody has access to it apart from you. The rest of the world is oblivious to the faith you share, and this makes it very dear to your heart. It can be put up anywhere in your private place. It could be on your shelf, reading table, or anywhere you deem fit. There are no rules to the right place to set up your private altar. In decorating your private Wiccan altar, you can put up symbols and images that make you feel comfortable. You do not have to worry about what anyone thinks or feels. Upon the private Wiccan altar type, it is absolutely permissible to keep the statutes of your patron gods and goddesses without any iota of doubt, fear or favor.

Coincidentally, a lot of pagans have private Wiccan altars but refuse to accept it as such. Inasmuch as people put up images of people they admire or idolize, they are also making use of the private Wiccan altar. The difference between the pagan style and the Wiccan practitioner style is that the later are able to accept who they are and work in that regard.

Ritual Wiccan altar:

The ritual Wiccan altar type is not to be erected at any place without due consideration. The name of the Wiccan altar type does not mean that it is only used for diabolic purposes. It is an altar style type that is used to achieve effective results, but it must be properly taken care of at all times. The striking difference between the home-based altar, the private altar, and the ritual altar is that the ritual altar is not displayed to the full glare of people. The ritual Wiccan altar must be kept clean at all times especially after a ritual has been performed on it.

This altar type must be structured in a way that the altar materials can be changed without encountering too much obstruction or difficulty. The location of the ritual altar determines the tools to use and how to set it up. If the ritual Wiccan altar is going to be used in a coven, then it is important to put the right materials that would aid its proper use in the coven. Though the ritual altar is used in performing rituals, the individuals who make use of the altar are in the best position to make decisions about how best to decorate the altar. As long as it suits the individual's needs, it is permissible.

One requirement of the location of the ritual Wiccan altar type is to get a comfortable location where the altar can be used very effectively to practice efficiently.

As much as the ritual Wiccan altar is used for rituals, it does not mean that it is the only Wiccan altar type that is used for rituals. As a matter of fact, the private Wiccan altar can also be used for ritual purposes or to cast spells. The only time when an individual may not use the private Wiccan altar to cast the spell is when the altar is too small. In cases like that, the individual is required to get a ritual Wiccan altar type to make optimum use of it for whatever reason.

CHAPTER - I
How to set up and care for the wiccan altar

This is a question that bothers a lot of people and leaves them utterly confused about how to go about it. Some individuals are very detailed and as such require details in setting up the Wiccan altar. The fact is; there are no definite rules to setting up the Wiccan altar. Just do what is right and makes your spirit relax!

The necessary steps to pay attention to are:

DECIDE ON THE LOCATION

In the previous chapter of this book, I explained in detail, the different types of altars that an individual may settle for. In all, there is a need to consider the location of the Wiccan altar. Do you want the Wiccan altar to be placed outside or inside your home? The answer to that question determines how you go about it. For individuals who have a garden, they may have a desire to feel closer to nature and taking up their spirituality a notch; this is absolutely normal. For people who do not have a garden, they will settle for indoor places. Even if the altar will be placed in the home, you need to decide on the exact room you want to situate your altar. This could be in the living room or your personal bedroom.

MAKE A DECISION ON THE DIRECTION OF THE ALTAR

The direction of the altar is sacrosanct. You need to understand the elements of nature and how to work with it. Some persons settle to face their altars in the east direction because the sun rises in the east. For others, the Northeast direction is a suitable position. They favor the argument that a lot of Wiccan practitioners always face the northeast when performing rituals. Nonetheless, an understanding of your personal element makes it easier for you to decide where your Wiccan altar should face.

DISCOVER A SUITABLE PLACE TO PUT YOUR ALTAR

 It is not enough to make decisions on the location of your altar or its direction. You also need to discover the place to keep your altar. There are lots of choices available at your disposal. You can decide to keep the altar on a bookshelf, drawers or any place you find suitable. Be guided by your instinct in making this decision. Remember, the altar defines your spirituality.

MAKE A CHOICE ON THE ALTAR TYPE

There are various altar types as clearly discussed in chapter one. The altar type you favor should reflect your purpose for setting up the altar. This also should be reflected in the symbols and images that you will use for your altar. Make these decisions carefully with an understanding that the altar reflects your spiritual practices and beliefs.

MAKE DECISIONS ON COLORS AND ITEMS TO USE

The items to be used are also very important. You need to understand that different items are used differently by the gods and goddesses. The different gods and goddesses symbolize different things and situations. Their significance must be adequately understood if you hope to get the best use from it. The colors as well must be adequately chosen in a way that expresses the intent behind the altar. Colors like blue, green and silver are regarded as the feminine color for the goddesses. For the gods, masculine colors are yellow, gold, orange and so on. More so, the different elements that represent masculine and feminine gods should also be encouraged.

POSITION OF THE ITEMS ON THE WICCAN ALTAR

The positions of the items are also very important in the Wiccan altar. It is not solely about getting the required items on the Wiccan altar. You need to also understand the positions of the items on your altar. All of the deity and spirit elements must be kept in the appropriate position so as to have the desired outcome of the spirituality or spiritual connection you seek. It is absolutely right to add any other items you feel is necessary on your altar. Remember, there are no concrete rules for setting up your name.

In setting up your Wicca altar, you need to understand the drive behind your intentions. The information you required is available at your disposal. All you need do is to listen to your inner spirit and let your instincts guide you. As long as it concerns your altar, you can never be wrong. Let your intuition direct you to do what is best for you. You should also be available to receive the counsel form your spirit.

24

CARE OF THE WICCAN ALTAR

The Wiccan altar has been likened to the heart of a human. The heart is protected with due diligence because from out of it comes the issues of life and death. The same way the heart is treated with utmost importance is the right way to handle the Wiccan altar.

Just like the heart, if the Wiccan altar is not properly cared for, the reason behind setting it up will not be actualized. The altar is a living entity. This is so because the altar harbors the presence of spiritual beings. If you do not take care of your body, what happens? Probably, the body would produce an offensive smell and would prevent people from associating with you. This same thing applies to the Wiccan altar. If it is not properly taken care of, it would make it difficult for your gods and goddesses to dwell within that altar.

Your altar is a sacred place and as such should be treated with the same understanding. Your Wiccan altar is capable of bringing forth something positive into your life and propelling you into achieving your life goals. But, none of this would be obtainable if you do not take proper care of your altar.

THE DANGERS OF NOT TAKING CARE OF YOUR ALTAR

There are always consequences attached to the negligence of duty. Yes, you heard correctly. It is your duty to take care of your altar. Remember, it was your personal decision to set up the altar for reasons best known to you. As such, you are responsible for what becomes of the altar. Let's do more practical work. Take a close look at the garden in your home. What do you observe? It is looking very beautiful, right? The flowers are probably very colorful and have attracted butterflies to suck from their petals. If you do not tend to the garden in about three months, what happens to it? Your guess is as good as mine. There would be a lot of overgrown leaves and some weeds. These unwanted plants would snatch away the essence of your garden and make it look unattractive; even the butterflies would find it difficult to perch on those flowers because of its state.

Consequently, when you do not take care of your Wiccan altar it becomes like an unattended garden. That is, it becomes unattractive, neglected and old. You must agree with me that going to a garden overgrown with weeds is almost impossible for anyone in their right senses. The same applies to the Wiccan altar. When you do not take proper care of the altar, it becomes difficult for you to make use of it. Even when you do, you don't get the same feeling you would originally do because of the state oof the altar. Just like the garden produces fresh, clean air and makes you healthy, a clean altar would do the same to your spirit.

CARING FOR THE WICCAN ALTAR

Now, you have realized the effect of neglecting your altar. I am very certain you now have the right understanding of where you get it all wrong. Not too worry, it is still very possible to do what is right. That is, taking care of the Wiccan altar.

The processes to this are actually very simple. Every Wiccan practitioner must bear this in mind at all times and act accordingly. Pay attention to these steps of caring for the Wiccan altar. They are:

ATTACH IMPORTANCE TO THE WICCAN ALTAR TOOLS

The Wiccan tools are actually very symbolic and as such are regarded with extreme importance. This presupposes that in choosing Wiccan tools you must attach importance and the right attitudes to get a suitable Wiccan altar tool. When you want to dispose of an old altar tool, you need to do it with an understanding of its sacredness. The fact that you had gotten a new replacement for the tool doesn't take away the relevance of the old altar tool. So, dispose of the old Wiccan altar tool respectfully. Then, when you get the new altar tool, it is necessary to dedicate the altar tool and consecrate it. To get the best of the new altar tool, purify the altar tool. Store the altar tools properly so as to avoid getting it all wrong.

KEEP THE ALTAR CLEAN AT ALL TIMES

The Wiccan altar is very essential because it is your personal way of communicating with your spirit. The Wiccan altar should be in the right state at all times. Whenever you notice that the altar is getting old, update it with the altar material. Clean the altar tools and dust it properly. The altar cloths should be adequately catered for. When it gets dirty, it should be washed properly. The candles as well should be replaced when they already getting old. Remember the popular saying" cleanliness is next to godliness", right? That is the case for the Wiccan altar. If you need the altar to remain in its sacred state, you need to keep it clean.

SPIRITUAL PRACTICES

The altar is a spiritual being and should be maintained in that status quo. The kind of spiritual practices that you employ at your altar place is very important in determining the content of the altar. Make appropriate sacrifices and offerings to the divinity that lies within the altar. The altar gods and goddesses should also be treated with the utmost respect. Ensure you take absolute care of the deities. Your altar is yours alone and should be treated with a sacred understanding. More so, you need to respect other people's altar as well. It is not only enough to respect your personal altar; you

28

need to respect others.

Additionally, anything that concerns the altar must be treated with a sense of responsibility. A nonchalant attitude is not to be encouraged at the Wiccan altar. It must be done with the utmost sense of responsibility and care.

THE IMPORTANCE OF KEEPING YOUR WICCAN ALTAR CLEAN

Asides from knowing the "How", it is also important to state the "Why". It is not just enough to state the processes of keeping the Wiccan altar clean, it is necessary to state the reasons behind such a notion.

It is a lot easier to get an action done when the reasons are clearly stated. Many a time, giving information without stating the significance of the information given doesn't make people attach much importance to the action. So, for the purpose of a clearer understanding, it is right to state those reasons behind keeping your Wiccan altar clean. Now, you may ask the question "Why do I need to keep my Wiccan altar clean?" You have the right to know the reason behind every action you take. So, for clarity purposes, this part of the book will provide the necessary details you seek.

The importance of keeping an altar clean is not really understood by a lot of people. Others may argue that since the altar is a personal decision, then, they are at the best positions to decide how to take care of such an altar. You may not be wrong in stating this fact but it erroneous to assume that the altar belongs to you solely. In the first chapter of this book, I had taken some time to explain that the Wiccan altar is not just about you but the existence and presence of some divine beings on the altar. So, the fact that you know so much about yourself doesn't mean you know about the other beings that are clearly invisible. To play safe, never be too quick to reach conclusions about certain issues especially when it revolves around divinity. It may seem right and normal to you to treat the altar the way that pleases you, but it doesn't make it the right thing to do.

There is nothing wrong in getting it wrong the first time, there is always room for the right things to be done. So, this next part of the book will clearly spell out the importance of a clean altar. I am sure you desire to know what these reasons are, right? Now, you have it!

THE FIRST IMPORTANCE OF KEEPING THE WICCAN ALTAR CLEAN IS TO ENERGIZE YOUR SPIRIT

An altar is not a plaything. Before you made the decision of having an altar, something must have prompted you. This reason is not solely because you want an altar but for the singular fact that you believe in the potency of the altar. It would be quite a pity if after going through the rigors of having an altar and purchasing the necessary altar tools you do not get the desired outcome from such an altar. Your altar is a channel between the physical and the spiritual. Remember,

30

upon the altar, you perform chants, prayers and other spiritual affairs. In the course of doing it, what happens to you? You are energized! You may not know it. But that is exactly what happens. It is impossible to derive energy from a dirty looking or unkempt altar. Instead of feeling energized, you would be weakened. The reality is not far- fetched. As long as the purpose behind setting up the altar is not established, the reverse becomes the case. To avert such circumstances, it becomes important to keep the altar clean at all times.

ANOTHER IMPORTANCE IS AN UNCLEAN ALTAR MAKES IT DIFFICULT FOR YOU TO MOVE FORWARD IN LIFE

Your altar is a symbol of your existence. All you ever wish to become and achieve is available within the arms of the altar. All you need do is to simply stretch forth your hand and reach for it. Can you remember how irritated you feel when you stretch forth your hand to receive a gift from a dirty outstretched hand? That is the same way it feels when you want to reach out to receive from a dirty altar. Irritation! You cannot move forward without keeping your altar clean. We have created a balance between you and the altar and have shown that you and the altar are two entwined entities. This implies that one cannot move forward without the other. The impression that you can achieve all you ever desire without considering the state of your altar is a painted truth. As a matter of fact, you are just scared to accept your reality. If your altar is not in good condition, that is the same way you are portrayed, and this would reflect in every aspect of your life. Do not be misguided! An altar that is plagued with old spells and symbols will not create the room for you to have good clear thoughts. How do you even think it is possible to have a proper state of mind when your altar is surrounded by too many old spells and symbols? Your altar is a spiritual representation of your physical being. So, keep it clean so as to forge ahead and do the exploits you so desire.

A DIRTY ALTAR HINDERS THE OPPORTUNITIES TO FOCUS CLEARLY

An altar that is cluttered hinders the presence of new things in your life. The state of the altar will impair with everything that concerns you. You would realize that you are experiencing a lot of difficult in being the person you want to be. Just as the altar is carelessly arranged that is the same way your priorities would look like. When your priorities are misplaced, you will realize that you can't do things the right way. You would experience difficulty in focusing your mind at a particular task and getting it done. This is so because you have failed to consider your altar a priority. As such, other priorities would never materialize. This is the reality of too many individuals who are Wiccan practitioners. They want the very best form the altar but fail at the simple task of keeping it clean. Before you quickly conclude that the altar is not working in your favor, pay attention to its state and decide if you have taken proper care of the altar before desiring such for your life.

AN UNCLEAN ALTAR CAUSES TOO MANY CHALLENGES

Undoubtedly, life is not a bed of roses. No one has proved that life would come without hassles. But rather than be a victim of hassles caused by spiritual entities, be contended with living a life without a personal altar. Inasmuch as the benefits of having an altar are tremendous, it is also the major factor behind challenges some individuals face. As a Wiccan practitioner, when the challenges are unseeingly greater than you have anticipated, quickly do an analysis of your life again. Your life is an expression of all that you represent and that includes your altar too. So, having a dirty altar is indirectly welcoming all manner of challenges into your life. These challenges may consume you if they are not properly handled using the right process. There are absolutely no difficulties in keeping your altar clean. It is synonymous to the way you care for your body and everything you hold dear. In all sincerity, it is rather unfair to neglect an altar you pray on and hope to get the best out of it. So, if you desire to live life with minimal challenges keeps your Wiccan altar clean.

A CLEAN ALTAR GUARANTEES THE ABSENCE OF A NEGATIVE RESULT

For everything you do in life, there would be a result of the sort. It could be negative or positive. The purpose of having a Wiccan altar is to get a positive result in every ramification of your life. When the altar feels neglected, it does the exact opposite of what you anticipated. This doesn't mean that the deities are unpleasant and inconsiderate, No. they actually feel just like humans do. A typical instance is a way you relate to your sibling at home. When your sibling fails to acknowledge your help and show kindness, how do you feel? I am sure the feeling is not a pleasant one. That is the same way it is for this immortal being. Come to think of it, you have an image of a deity on your altar. What do you think it means? It is a physical representation of the spiritual being you cannot see. So, when you make your prayers or say your chants, the physical image of the god and goddess actually sees you. For every promise and vow you make before them, they take a record of it. The fact that you don't see it doesn't mean it is false. The adverse effect of this is that when you go contrary to the things you say before them, they make you pay for it. And trust me, you would pay dearly. Now, the way the altar functions is that irrespective of its state, whether clean or dirty, they provide results. The major difference is that in the case of a dirty altar, the results are not beneficial to you.

TAKE CARE OF YOUR ALTAR

All of this importance of keeping the Wiccan altar clean is to be taken very seriously. A dirty or outdated altar does more good than harm. Don't ever assume that having an altar keeps off bad things from you. The truth is your altar can actually attract bad things your way depending on its state. If you want to get the best form your employer at work, what do you do? Simply put, you please them and give them reasons to make you happy. The altar works in the same light. To get the best form your altar, you must keep it clean at all times and do whatever it takes to keep the altar decoration intact. In the earlier part of this book, we likened the altar to a garden. In that, a beautiful garden attracts butterflies to aid its pollination system. So also the Wiccan altar attracts the deities that are charged with the responsibility of helping you come to be the best that you are.

Caring for the Wiccan altar doesn't require a lot of work and resources. With the limited resources you have, you can actually bring out the best from your altar. Pay attention to what you can afford. Don't decorate an altar the way you cannot afford because subsequently, it would require an upgrade. The upgrade is usually necessary so as to improve the state and physical outlook of the altar. Your Wiccan altar mirrors the content of your soul. The soul is a weapon that determines quite a number of actions you take; be it good or bad. The Wiccan altar as well helps to control the actions that are acted upon in the soul. Whatever you feel should be reflected in the way your altar looks at a certain point in time. You and your altar share a deeper connection than you even realize. Your emotions are really important when addressing your altar. Resist the desire to neglect the altar because you feel you are in control. You are not in control. You are just the person who is expected to care for the altar. Like every organization pays wages to workers, when you do what is expected of you, your wages will be paid in full and trust me when I saw, you would actually love to be rewarded in the right way.

NONE OF THIS IS A REALITY IF THE ALTAR IS NOT PROPERLY CARED FOR IN THE RIGHT WAY. HENCE, YOU NEED TO UNDERSTAND THE REASON FOR CARING FOR YOUR ALTAR SO AS TO CONSIDER IT A VERY IMPORTANT ISSUE.

CHAPTER - 2
What to know before you start

WHAT TO DO AND WHAT TO NOT DO ON A WICCAN ALTAR

The Wiccan altar is guided by a lot of regulations and every Wiccan practitioner is expected to comply with these instructions so as to achieve a considerable level of desired results.

The Wiccan altar embodies a lot of spiritual-related activities and it is important to reverence the altar. The reason a lot of practitioners may not get the desired result of all they intend to achieve is probably because they failed to do what is expected of them.

Some of the do's and don'ts of the Wiccan altar includes but not limited to:

WHAT TO DO

Keep the Wiccan altar clean at all times

Whenever a spell or ritual has been carried out on the altar ensure to clean it up and perform the necessary cleansing ritual before commencing with a new spell.

Get the appropriate tools for the altar

The tools are very essential for the Wiccan practice. Ensure to get the right kind of tools for any spell or ritual to be conducted.

Ensure to wear the appropriate outfit on the altar

Inasmuch as the practitioners or witches are allowed to wear any type of clothing, on the Wiccan altar, they are expected to put on the appropriate dress or robes for the spell they intend to carry out.

Make use of spells on the altar

The use of spells on the Wiccan altar is highly permissible. Witches and practitioners are allowed to make use of spells for their rituals and offerings. In this vein, there are lots of spells and it is best to use the appropriate spell that suits the ritual.

You can make use of magic wands

On the Wiccan altar, it is highly suitable to make use of the magic wands. The magic wands are used to channel energy and also for healing purposes.

The Wiccan altar can be used for religious practices

Just like other religious beliefs make use of altars for their religious purposes, the Wiccan altar also serves as a means of religious practice. As such, it can be used for religious benefits and purposes.

WHAT NOT TO DO

The Wiccan altar is not used for evil purposes:

The Wiccan religion doesn't encourage the use of evil purposes and intentions. Even in the use of spells and rituals, it is not used to manipulate or cause harm to another person. For this reason, the Wiccan altar is not to be used to bring harm to another individual. Rather, it is to be used to make them become better or positive minded.

The Wiccan altar is not to promote Satanism:

The religion itself does not promote any satan- related activities. Contrary to what a lot of people think, religion is used to promote balance in nature, and this is achieved by using some natural elements. To this effect, they make use of different gods and goddesses and make the appropriate type of prayers to these deities.

The Wiccan altar is not to be treated with disrespect:

The altar is regarded as sacred. As such, it should be treated with the utmost reverence. It is not proper to allow anyone to desecrate your altar. It is yours and you have the responsibility of keeping it in its rightful state.

CHAPTER - 3
How the magic ritual with a wicca altar works

The Wicca religion is quite different from the contemporary religions. Unlike the contemporary religion, there are specified buildings, doctrines, temples and books to use for religious practices. But, in Wiccan, the reverse is the case. There are no definite rules to follow in terms of praying and the different Wiccan practitioners can practice the religion the way they deem fit. There are no specified rules for religion.

Additionally, there are no historical facts to fall back on as is commonly seen ion most religious beliefs. Wiccan religion is an evolving religion, but it is gradually gaining grounds in society. The practitioners are increasing by the day and it is considered an essential kind of religion. One unique thing that Wicca shares with other religion are the use of an altar. No religion functions properly without an altar. The altar is considered an essential praying ground where answers to requests and heart desires are met. The various altars in the too many religions in the world today make use of sacred objects and images on their altar. These images are considered a physical representation of the gods and goddesses they believe in. it is a medium for the practitioners to communicate and adore the presence of their gods upon the altar.

The Wiccan altar is considered a sacred place where different rituals can be carried out. The rituals of sabbats and Esbats are usually performed on the Wiccan altar. Any other ritual the practitioner desires to carry out can be effectively done on the Wiccan altar. Whoever that wishes to participate in the Wiccan religion must fully understand what it entails to carry on with the religious beliefs as well as understand how the altar works for magic.

SOME TOOLS NEEDED FOR THE RITUAL ON THE WICCAN ALTAR ARE:

- Candles
- Chalice
- Athame
- Bell
- Besom
- Book of shadows
- Cauldron
- Crystals
- Divination methods
- Pentacle

- Robe
- Staff
- Wand

CANDLES

These candles are very sacrosanct tools for performing rituals on the altar. They are symbolic of honoring the gods and goddesses. If you want to perform a ritual and hope to get the result, it is important to honor and appreciate the gods and goddesses who are responsible for assisting you with your intentions. This can only be possible when you honor their presence or acknowledge their benevolence by putting on a candle.

Candles are tools that belong to the element of fire. The belief behind this tool is that the fire would drain you of your personal energy and then release the energy at a suitable time when you need it the most. They are functional in activating spells to work effectively. Another thing that is taken quite seriously in performing rituals on the Wiccan altar is the color of the candle. It is believed that certain colors are used to represent different situations and ritual type. It is absolutely permissible to make your own candles for ritual. Some practitioners are of the opinion that making personal candles for ritual purposes is more effective than the candle that is bought. While some other individuals argue against such theory and concluded that it is not a function of how the candle was made or where it was purchased. According to the latter group, the candles efficiency is solely a factor of the energy level that was committed to seeing the ritual work. Whatever be the case, the fact remains that candles are extremely important and is the most popular tool for performing rituals.

CHALICE

This is a tool that is closely similar to the cauldron. Just like the cauldron, it is used for goddess-oriented traditions. It is womb-like and is regarded as a tool where life begins. It also signifies the element of water on the altar. On some altars, the chalice is used alongside the athame to represent the feminine part of a divine being. There are no rules to the right kind of material for the chalice. It can be of any material that suits your preferences. It could be silver, pewter or ceramic. Although in recent times, a lot of people have favored the ceramic material of the chalice compared to the pewter or silver material because it is readily available During rituals, the chalice is usually passed around the practitioners in the circle to create ease for them sip the wine. This is usually referred to as a bonding process for the practitioners in that its unities them and creates a sense of belonging among the participants. After sipping the wine from the chalice, the practitioners would speak their best wishes to each other. Such as "May you never thirst!"

ATHAME

This is a significant tool for ritual on the Wiccan altar.
It is used for channeling energy. In performing rituals,
you would surely need to channel energy and to do this
you need an athame on your altar. This tool is necessary when casting a circle for the ritual. It looks more
like a dagger that has a double edge. The athame can be
substituted for a wand.it doesn't necessarily mean that
the athame is used for cutting anything. It is just symbolic of energy and its appearance doesn't represent
anything violent. This tool can be made by yourself if
you want to minimize costs. It can also be purchased.
But, one thing is pertinent. This tool is indispensable
in performing rituals on the altar.

BELL

The bell is symbolic for generating sound. These
sounds are a great way of driving away unwanted presence and bad energies. It is also used to honor the
gods and goddesses and recognize their importance to
the ritual you want to carry out. The sound from the
bell generates vibration and also is interrelated with
various parts such as the singing bowl or ritual rattle.
The coordination of all of these parts helps to create a
harmony that is essential in the magical circle.
Sometimes, the bell is rung just before a ritual rite begins or at the end of the ritual. To some practitioners,

the bell is rung to honor the dead people and to do this, the bell should be rung for about forty (40) times. For the purposes of ritual, the bell can also be used with the athame. That is, the athame can be used to hit the bell to produce the desired sound.

BESOM

It is notable for one important function. That is, to cleanse the space that would be used for the ritual. It is used in cleaning out the area where the ritual will be performed. It is important to reiterate that rituals in the Wiccan altar are not to be treated very lightly. It is a serious issue and should be treated with a sense of urgency and deep commitment. Prior to this chapter, I explained how to take care of the Wiccan altar and the importance of a clean altar. This explains that the Wiccan ritual is no joke at all! Additionally, this tool is used to rid the area of any negative energy that may have occupied the place after the last ritual. Suffice to say, the ritual space must be cleaned with the besom before and after a ritual is performed.

It is also important to note that a besom is a ritual tool that is connected to the water element. There are a lot of Wiccan practitioners and witches who make use of besom. This is because they understand the importance and relevance of the tool. Some practitioners may not have what it takes to afford the besom. As such, they settle for making their own besom. The necessary material required to make a besom is a staff of ash, some bundle of birch twig and so on.

BOOK OF SHADOWS

Inasmuch as there are no complete documents of the book of shadows, this tool is still held in esteemed reverence. In the Wiccan religion, the book of shadows is a book that contains the information on the spells, information, correspondence, ritual types and the rules governing magic. All of the information contained in the book of the shadow is extremely important. It is not possible to perform a ritual without knowing the right spells to chant and when to say them. This book of the shadow is usually transferred from one generation to the next so as to teach the right values to the younger generation. To the Wiccan practitioners, the book of the shadow is regarded to be an esteemed tool and it reflects their very personal information and details

CAULDRON

This tool is regarded as a tool where life begins. It is feminine and is attached to the goddess. It is similar to the chalice in that it is mostly used in goddess- an oriented type of tradition and tradition. It looks more like a female womb and is regarded as a womb-like tool. The cauldron ritual tool is an element of water. Some proponents have brought up an argument for the cauldron tool. They argued this by stating that the cauldron tool is closely related to Cerridwen. Cerridwen is a goddess who is believed to have the power of prophecy and an inspiration to so many especially the underworld.

The cauldron has too many uses and benefits. Some of the uses of the cauldron are a tool for burning candles or offering sacrifices on them, burn incense, representative of the goddess of your tradition or belief, for blending herbs that are needed for magical works and lastly to use it as a tool for filling water and scrying during the moonlight.

The ritual- based cauldron should be separated from a cooking cauldron. Both should not be used interchangeably. In cases where the cauldron is made from cast iron, it should be properly seasoned so as to prevent getting a rusty shape and look.

CRYSTALS

There are a lot of different crystals that are used for ritual purposes. The use of these crystals depends on the intention of the practitioner. Whatever the practitioners decide to use the crystals for depending on the choice of crystals he would make. Nonetheless, it is necessary to choose crystals based on their attributes and significance. If you desire to get the best from a ritual performed with a crystal, understand the type of crystal to use and its correspondence. In that way, you will never be wrong with the choice you have made. Fortunately, crystals can be substituted for birth months. Each birth month has a unique stone that should be used to get the best out of it. These stones possess magical qualities that must be used judiciously to get the very best. Also, after purchasing a new crystal stone, ensure you do not make use of it except after cleansing it. You need to cleanse the new crystal stone before you can make use of it.

DIVINATION METHODS

There are different methods that are used for divination purposes. Any divination method you adopt should reflect your abilities and competence. A lot of people like to try all manner of divination methods. But, if you look at yourself very closely, you will discover that you are very competent in a particular method than the others. The best thing is to stick to a method you are very comfortable and competent with. The ritual doesn't entail doing all sorts of practice and methods. No. Simply stick to the method that suits you and your abilities. There are various divination methods like reading tarot cards, ogham staves, pendulum, Norse runes. If you are good at one of these divination methods, then there is really no need trying out other methods. Stick to the method that makes you feel comfortable the most.

PENTACLE

The pentacle is very different from the pentagram. Virtually all Wiccan rituals make use of the pentacle. The pentacle is recognized as a flat piece of material such as paper, wood, clay or any material that is inscribed with some magical symbols. It is otherwise known as a representative of earth. On certain occasions, the pentacle functions as a talisman especially for ceremonial purposes. More so, the pentacle is symbolic on the altar as it is used for holding down materials to be consecrated in place. It can either be locally made or purchased from anywhere you deem right.

ROBE

The robe is attire that is worn by a practitioner when it is time for a ritual to be performed. The robe is very popular in different religions. Almost all practitioners of different religions wear robes especially to commemorate an activity or function. The same applies to the Wiccan ritual. For the Wiccan ritual, robes are worn depending on the type of ritual to be carried out. Different colors of robe symbolize the kind of ritual to be done. If the ritual is to be performed in a coven, then, the members of the coven will be required to put on the same color of a robe for all practitioners.

Additionally, the color of the robe can also be worn to indicate the position or height a practitioner has attained. The robe is usually worn by practitioners to create a sense of responsibility and to differentiate the activity from the normal day's activity. When practitioners wear a robe for ritual purposes, their mindset is drawn to the importance of the ritual and its symbolic representation. There are rules on how to dress beneath the robe. If you feel comfortable naked underneath the robe, then do it. As long as it makes you feel comfortable, there are no restrictions on what you wear beneath your robe.

STAFF

The staff is a ritual tool that is used to draw energy. It is not a compulsory ritual tool, unlike the others. But it can also be important in certain ritual types. The staff is symbolic of authority. As such, it is necessary to understand how to make use of it. Many a time, the only people who are authorized or permitted to carry the staff are the priest or priestess of the altar. It can either symbolize air or water. It depends on the context it was used. It represents male energy and is regarded as a masculine tool. The staff can be made by anyone or can be purchased according to what you intend to do.

WAND

One of the most popular tools for ritual purposes or in the Wiccan ritual purposes is the wand. If you want to direct energy during the ritual purposes, the best tool to use is the wand. It is regarded as masculine because it represents male energy and virility. It can either represent air or water. In ritual purposes, the wand can be used to invoke a deity or to duly consecrate a sacred environment. There are different materials that can be used to make the wand. These materials can either be any metal, copper, glass or wood. In all, the choice material for making a wand is the wood. These woods have different magical significance and use. It is possible for a practitioner or witch to have different kinds of wands according to their needs. These magical wands are necessary to symbolize the importance of different rituals. However, witches would rather favor a wand than an athame.

All of these tools are needed to connect the practitioner with the altar. Virtually all, if not all individuals have an innate power within them to command result. The only thing needed is the ability to do what is necessary on the altar. The results that are desired are within their immediate reach. They only need to look within and find out how to use the powers that are already deposited in them.

52

PREPARATION FOR A WICCAN RITUAL

Everything action that is carried out in life requires a process. This is the same for the Wiccan ritual. Inasmuch as there are no "right" ways of preparing for the ritual, it is necessary to do what you think is right. Preparing for the ritual is considered very essential in the Wiccan religion. This is to equip the practitioner with the ideal mindset to commence the rituals.

The first thing to be done in preparing for the Wiccan ritual is to purify oneself. Before the ritual begins, the practitioner or witch needs to purify the circle with a besom. This is done by sweeping the area carefully. Also, the witch purifies herself or himself using incense over her/his body. When purifying the area, the witch places the besom over his/her hand and walks in spiral patterns on the circle. Such individual also halts at four quadrant points. The second thing the practitioner does is to set up the altar facing the east side. Such an altar would also be graced with water and salt which would be used for purification purposes. The candles should also be mounted on the altar to signify the presence of the gods and goddesses. Furthermore, candles are to be placed at the four points of the circle. Next, the circle is cast. The circle is considered very essential in performing rituals and a lot of relevance is attached to it. The materials needed for casting the circles are the athame, wand or staff. The circle is regarded as a point that is void of time. The area where the circle is cast is also purified again using salt and water. Then, the person who wants to perform the ritual places three pinches of salt into some quantity of water; stirs it nine times with the aid of an athame and uses it to purify the area. After this, incense is lit and carried around the perimeter of the circle. The third step is to summon the various elements. The various elements are water, earth, fire, and air. These elements are regarded as the guardian of the practitioners.

Magic is incomplete with the permission of the deity. So, the deity is invoked to ensure that the ritual goes as planned. The deities are summoned or invoked by reciting certain chants. This deity can either be a male (god) or female (female). It depends on the type of ritual to be performed.

PERFORMING THE ACTUAL RITUAL

A very common type of ritual in the Wiccan altar is the great rite ritual. This ritual is usually performed by the priest and priestess at the Wiccan altar. The Great rite ritual is referred to as a sexual union between the god and goddess to bring in a new kind of energy that promotes a ripe and good harvest. There are two ways of performing the great rite. It could be carried out in a symbolic manner such as the union between the ritual tools like the athame and cauldron or between the priest and the priestess. Whatever form the sexual union will take must be mutually agreed upon by the members of the coven. The sexual union is usually conducted in private without the presence of the other members of the union. In most cases, the priest and priestess are always married.

Though, the most favored sexual union of the great rite ritual is the symbolic ritual where the priest and priestess make use of various symbols. In fulfillment of this sexual union, the cauldron is held by the priestess. The cauldron has a womb-likee a shape and is regarded as being feminine while the priest holds the athame. Then, the priestess kneels with the cauldron in her hands facing the priest and the priest also faces her with his athame. The priest and the priestess recite lines to invoke the god (the sun king) and goddesses (maiden of spring). After which the priest would lower his athame to meet with the cauldron and both parties recite chants from the land of youth and the wine of life. After doing this, the high priest of the altar holds up the cauldron and announces that the rite symbolizes the union of the god and goddess. Immediately the ritual has been performed, the circle is closed.

In closing the circle, the priest or priestess appreciates the gods and goddess for their help, the quarters are released and the high priest in charge takes down the circle with the athame pointed facing outside.

CHAPTER - 4
Intermediate spells for wicca altar

Wiccan spells are regarded as the safest type of spells.

These spells are rid of negative energies and influence over anyone. With the Wiccan spell, it is easier to bring forth anything the practitioner desire without experiencing so much of a problem. These sorts of spells are usually cast by a Wiccan practitioner or witch. In some cases, most practitioners or witches that are not Wiccan also make use of the spells.

What does cast a spell means? Casting a spell is basically gathering spiritual energies and converting them into something more. That is, being in possession of energies that you can send forth into the universe so as to create a change. It is pertinent to note that casting a spell can have its repercussion. This is so because there are various elements that are involved in the process. So, once the chant has been pronounced and the spell has been cast, it is difficult if not possible to cause the spell to be revoked. So, to play safe, it is better to understand the consequences of each spell before casting it.

Hence, it is important to weigh your reasons before casting a spell. More so, you should be adequately prepared for the repercussions if any should come up.

PROTECTION SPELL

The protection spell is a type of spell that protects individuals from negative and unwanted energies. There are always a large number of negative energies that can affect an individual's life. This type of spell ensures that individuals are rid of the effects of vices such as jealousy, envy, greed, sorcery and so on.

Items needed are

- A personal picture
- Five candles (Four Blue and one white)
- Oil that suits your astrological sign
- Incense for purification
- Acacia leaves
- Tourmaline stones

How to cast the spell

- Cleanse yourself with some quantity of water that contains a drop of your essential oil. In cases where there is no essential oil, the practitioner can improvise by adding some quantity of salt to the water and washing with it.
- Then, prepare to cast the circle. To do this, place one of the four blue candles at the four cardinal points while the white candle should be placed in front of you.
- The incense should be kept at the left side of the white candle and the tourmaline stones should be

kept at the right.
- Put your personal picture in front of the white candle
- Now, cast the circle for the ritual and light the incense as well
- Place your personal picture three times over the incense and envision yourself being cleansed from all the unwanted energies around you.
- The next step is to use the acacia leaves and tourmaline stone and place it in your hands while reciting these chants five times "I invoke thee Aradia, goddess of protection and healing. Protect me and keep me safe now and forever. I thank you and I release you"
- After which you will visualize a circle moving around you. Send forth your love, healing, and energies into it so as to make it grow.
- Get rid of those unwanted energies and put off your candles.
- Now, close the circle and let the incense burn out in order to complete the process.

Advantages of the protection spell

- The spell can bring about positive responses from the practitioner's life
- It is a protective spell that is used to protect you and your loved ones away from harm
- The spell doesn't cause harm to anyone

Disadvantages of the protection spell

- This spell requires being cast by an experienced practitioner. In the case where the individual is not experienced, the spell may not work.

- It requires caution because of the effect of the three-fold return
- It is not as powerful as the dark magic spells of protection

GODDESS PROTECTION SPELL

This spell is very potent and powerful. This spell is very simple and is actually done by mentally visualizing a blue colored light surrounding you wherever you are. The moment you stop focusing on the incantation, it stops being effective.

Repeat this incantation:

> "GREAT GODDESS OF DAY AND NIGHT,
> PROTECT ME WITH ALL MY MIGHT"

A spell made against outside influence: This spell is used to protect your mind and thoughts from individuals who may attempt to influence your thoughts and words

Just recite this incantation:

> ""IN THIS PLACE AND HOUR, BY THE GUARDIANS
> AND THE SECRET OF THE NIGHT, TAKE THE KEYS TO
> MY HEART AND CLOSE THE DOORS OF MY MIND"

62

GOLDEN MIST SHIELD SPELL

This spell is used most times when you are surrounded by negative people and don't want to be influenced by the content of their being. It creates an aura around the practitioner and acts as a shield that obstructs negative thoughts and words. This spell also helps to eliminate negativity. Whenever you discover you are surrounded by negative people, this spell is always very effective and doesn't cause any discomfort of any kind. However, this spell doesn't protect against demonic attacks and curses. Hence, it is always prone to dissipate when there are instances of curses or other demonic related activities.

The incantation to be made is:

"THE BREATH OF LIFE, THE LIGHT OF MY MIND, CREATES AN ENCHANTMENT OF PROTECTION AND COMFORT, LIKE THE AIR I BREATHE IS PURIFIED, I SURROUND MYSELF WITH AN ORB OF GOLD, THIS GOLDEN HAZE IS CONSTANTLY PURIFIED AND SEPARATED FROM ANY NEGATIVITY, MAY MY SPACE BE PROTECTED"

LOVE SPELLS

Love spells are basically the most popular type of Wiccan spell. The good about the Wiccan love spell is that it doesn't really force the person into loving you. It could be purposed to make the person a better person or to shine brightly in all ramifications of life. It isn't solely basic on intimate relationships. In casting a love spell, caution is required! There are terrible situations where after casting the love spell, you may realize the person isn't the exact kind of person you had hoped to fall in love with. In such situations, what do you do?

Different types of love spells

- Candle spells
- Potions
- Written spells
- Fragrance oil
- Voodoo love spells
- Flower love spell

All of the aforementioned types of love spells are very potent and magical. They also possess their own repercussions and are considered very dangerous. One good fact about the Wiccan spell is that it is not intended to harm anyone and doesn't manipulate others into doing things that are against their will. Some proponents of love spell have argued that there is absolutely nothing wrong in causing people to act against their will by giving them various gift items. They argue it is similar to the popular seduction act where people dress provocatively to attract people they desire.

The Wiccan love spell is usually cast upon an individual you feel attracted to and want them to feel the same towards you. The major significance is that the spell doesn't affect their will to live life in a manner that pleases them. It only acts as a spiritual connection between both parties that are involved. It cleanses them of negative or contrary energy. More like it cleanses the spiritual pathway of both individuals and gives them a deeper sense of connection. Though, nobody's will is affected.

The ideal time for casting a love spell is at night, on Fridays and also at the full moon. The potency of the spell is better activated at this time.

Items that are needed

- Cauldron / ashtray / copalera
- Piece of paper
- A red-colored pen
- Four red colored candles
- Rose quartz/ Rose orgonite

How to cast the spell

- The first step is to cast the circle
- Then, place the red colored candles at the four cardinal points
- Lit up the cauldron
- With the aid of red ink, draw a heart symbol

and inscribe the name of the person you wish to send the beam of love to

• Place the rose quartz in your hand and visualize them sending their love beam across to you as well.

• Place your lips on the paper and kiss the inscribed name three times

• Next, place the paper in burning fire and let it burn out thoroughly

"MY HEART ABLAZE AND SHINNING, THIS LOVE I DO SEND TO THEE, IF YOU FIND A PLACE IN YOUR HEART TO LOVE ME, BY THE GREATEST GOOD, SO MOTE IT IS"

The above words should be repeated three different times

After reciting it three times, close the circle and keep the rose quartz with you for at least a full moon cycle.

66

TWO HALVES WHOLE LOVE SPELL

This type of Wicca spell doesn't totally comply with the rules that govern casting a Wiccan love spell. It is a type of love spell that is targeted at bringing back one's love. There may be consequences attached to this spell be ready to accept its consequences if any.

This spell is better to cast on a waxing moon when the energies are at its peak or on a Friday night

Items that are needed are

- Two pictures of you and your ex-partner
- Athame/ kitchen knife
- Red-colored candle
- Black colored candle
- Coriander seeds
- Charcoal tablet

How to cast the spell

- Cast the circle
- Put on the red candle on your left side
- Put on the black candle on your right side
- Lit the charcoal at the center
- Sprinkle some quantity of coriander seed into the charcoal and allow it to produce smoke
- With the athame or kitchen knife, cut the picture into two parts and say these words:

> **RENT AND TORN**
> **LOVE'S FORLORN**
> **BROKEN APART**
> **BROKEN HEART**

- Hold the different parts of the picture over the smoke from the coriander
- Repeat the above chants again
- Put the pictures together so that they can overlap each other
- Put some black wax on both picture parts so as to bind them together
- Put some red wax over the black wax

Place the repaired photo over the smoke from the coriander and chant again:

> **BY THE MORN**
> **LOVE REBORN**
> **PIECED TOGETHER**
> **NOW AND FOREVER**

The last step is to put out the candles and leave the picture in between the candles until your ex-partner returns to your bosom

VOODOO LOVE SPELLS

Voodoo is a ritual act that is hinged on the belief that that magical act can be incorporated into the world. Voodoo love spells to tie a person to you. Whoever you want to make a spiritual connection with, the voodoo love spell can create such energy for the expected connection. It is entirely in line with the Wiccan love spell, but it does not also relate to black magic in whatever way. Voodoo has its own advantages and disadvantages in that it can restrict the use of someone's will. But it is not entirely as bad as people make it look like.

One distinguishing feature of this love spell with the other types of love spell is that it requires you to make use of a personal item of the person you wish to attract. When you are able to get a personal item of the individual you wish to attract, it makes the spell more potent. It is not entirely important to get a personal belonging of the person you hope to attract. As long as you can adequate use of your visualization and the intensity of your purpose, the spell can be cast.

This spell should be cast on the night of a waxing moon or on a Friday night. It is believed that these days are dedicated to the goddess of love.

Items that are needed are

- An unclean shirt of your intended partner
- Some strands of hair from the intended partner
- How to cast the spell

- Cleans your mind, your body, and your spirit
- Craft the desired poppet out of the unclean cloth of your intended partner
- Place the strands of hair of your intended partner on the poppet
- Place any additional material you have of your intended partner on the doll
- Any other additional material you have such as blood, nails and so on of your intended partner should be attached to the poppet
- Place the doll close to your bedside where you live. N.B: this would not cause any harm to come to your intended partner.
- Whenever you lay down close to the doll, speak to it just as you would talk to your intended partner. Your desired partner will hear and feel you irrespective of the distance between both of you.

Note: Any poppet that you make use of should be kept properly and in a safe place. Keep it away from pets and from the reach of children. Whenever you are not making use of it, keep away in a safe place.

The advantages of love spell

- Wiccan love spells are very potent and powerful
- It provides a variety of options for you to choose from
- It provides an avenue for people to meet their one true love

The disadvantages of love spell

- The consequences are usually grave especially when you find out that you are not compatible with such an individual.
- In some cases, it becomes difficult to separate both parties
- It could also be used to restrict someone's will. This is because the spell doesn't consider the other person's interest and feelings.

WICCAN SPELL FOR HARMONY AND BALANCE IN SPACE

This kind of spell is necessitated by the need to achieve balance in an environment. The spell provides the avenue to create balance in a small space. This could either be in the room, kitchen or even in your closet. Additionally, it can be used in an outdoor environment as long as the environment is not too big.

This spell makes use of flowers. For the purpose of casting the spell, the chants are enchanted into the flowers. Should the flowers be in the home, it is advisable to get a plant pot and keep the flowers. If the spell is for the outdoor space, after the spell has been cast, the flowers should be buried into the soil.

Items that are needed are

- Flowers
- Rosemary
- Thyme
- Cinnamon

How to cast the spell

- The first step is to cast the circle with your

flowers in the circle
- Then, sprinkle some quantity of thyme, cinnamon, and rosemary on the soil
- Make the following chants after sprinkling the cinnamon, thyme, and rosemary.
- "Balance and harmony, peacefulness and ease, by the power of the three, all turbulence of ease"
- Now, visualize peace and harmony going into the flowers
- Close your circle and keep the flower at the exact spot you wish to bring peace and harmony.

This spell for harmony and balance will only be effective as long as the flowers are still blooming. The moment the flowers wither away, the potency of the spell will be neutralized. So, you may have to cast another spell again after you notice that the flowers are withered away.

It should be noted that the spell can only be effective when there are persons who agree for such a spell to take place. That is, there should be at least an individual who desires to experience genuine harmony in the environment. In situations where there are persons who do not entirely want harmony and balance, the spell will not be effective.

WICCAN SPELLS TO STOP DRINKING ALCOHOL

This spell is cast to help an individual reduce his/ her intake of alcohol. The spell is best performed during a new moon.

Before casting the spell, it is important to think about your actions. Do you really want to cast the spell? Why do you want to cast the spell? Whatever your reasons are< write it down on a piece of paper. But, each of your reasons should be written down on a separate sheet of paper.

Items you will need are

- Small pieces of paper
- Pen
- An empty bottle and lid of your favorite alcoholic drink
- A string
- Bottle of water
- Orgonite

How to cast the spell

- The first step is to cast the circle. Before casting the circle, it is essential to ensure that you already have a clear mind and head. Mediate all that your reasons are, pick up the sheet of paper that contains your reasons and read them out aloud. After doing that, reaffirm the opposite of the reasons and accept that you are no longer addicted to alcoholic drinks.

• After making a positive declaration, appreciate the sincerity of the words you have spoken and then meditate on how you would feel with such newness. Perceive yourself to be in a different light, where you are entirely free from drinking alcohol. I appreciate how you feel after stopping alcoholic drinks. Put the piece of paper in your hand into the empty bottle you are holding

• Repeat the same process for every piece of paper that contains your reason. When you have placed every piece of paper into the bottle, cover the bottle with the lid.

• With the aid of the black cord, tie the bottleneck and secure it using three knots

• Take up a glass of water and imagine a white beaming light emanating from it. Now, drink the water contained in the glass and imagine the light seeping into your body.

• Embrace the purifying feel of the water as you drink it.

• Lastly, take the omegorite and place it between your hands. Embrace the feel of the white light as it surrounds your body making you feel stronger as the light flows into your body. Imagine the rays of the light going into the omegorite. Accept the totality of the process and do not stop until your instincts reveal that the process has been completed.

Chant these words:

"I AM NOW A NO-DRINKER. SO MOTE IT BE"

Accept the reality of the spoken words.

Close the circle. Get a suitable place for you to bury the bottle or discard it wherever you deem fit.

After performing the spell, carry the omegorite with you and whenever the urge to drink alcoholic drink comes, repeat the above steps and visualize a better version of yourself.

SPELL TO CAST AWAY BAD LUCK

Whenever you experience too many misfortunes all in a day, then it is important to get an anti-bad luck spell. There is every bit of a possibility that what is happening around you is no longer considered as normal and might possibly be a worrisome situation. This spell ensures that luck is restored with you and everything returns to normalcy around you. One notable feature of this spell is that if the bad luck was placed upon you by any individual, it uplifts the curse but doesn't affect the person who has placed the curse. It is not a revengeful spell and promotes forgiveness in place of revenge.

Items that are needed are

- Black parchment
- Black pen
- A green candle
- Cauldron

How to cast the spell

- The right way to go about this is to thoroughly clean out your room, house, workplace or any other place you feel is surrounded by negative energy
- Using the blank parchment, write out everything you think is a possible cause of the bad luck you have been experiencing or the incidents

that are responsible for the bad luck
- Put on the candle and burn out the blank parchment with the flames from the candle.
- Drop it on the fireproof bowl
- When the flame from the candle is burning out the blank parchment, recite these chants:

Misfortunes from the recent past are burning now
They will not last
- Last step is to put out the candle

A JOB PROMOTION SPELL

Job promotion spell is essential when you feel that you are overdue for a job promotion, but it is not forthcoming. This spell ensures that you advance in your career path, get a better-paid job or even get an increase in your salary. Fortunately, the universe is equipped with the power to make it a reality.

However, this spell is only potent when you have been putting insufficient energy levels into the job. It doesn't work when you are idle or not making the necessary efforts. In situations when you are not putting in the desired effort, the spell can have an aftermath effect on you.

Items that are needed are

- Row rolled oats
- Beeswax candle
- Bay leaves
- Clay pot

How to cast the spell

- Get a quiet suitable environment. Sit on the floor of the preferred environment. You may also settle for a cushion but avoid sitting on a chair.
- With your eyes shut tight, focus on how much effort you have put into your job and what you have achieved so far.
- Embrace the warmth that courses through your

vein together with the satisfaction that you feel

• Now, open your eyes and take some quantity of rolled oats into your hands. Throe it into the clay pot and put it on a candle and place it close to the clay pot. Put the bay leaves close to the clay pot and say this incantation for three times:

• Money, prosperity, wealth, recognition
• May my career reach the state of ignition
• Shut your eyes for the second time and medita-te on yourself accepting anew promotion, job or an increased paycheck. Let your thoughts be centered on the feel it brings your way.

• Ensure you don't put out the candle. It is totally acceptable to change its position but does not put it out. Allow it to burn out completely. After this happens, clean out the installation

SPELL FOR A SUCCESSFUL DIVOR-CE

Divorce is always considered to be difficult for both parties involved. It requires a lot of energy, resources and leaves a number of hopes shattered and hearts are broken. These are some of the reasons it is mostly difficult to go on with divorce situations. Inasmuch as divorce comes with a lot of pain and difficult legal processes, this spell ensures that the divorce ends very successful with little difficulties. This spell is usually aimed at reducing or eliminating the burden that comes with divorce. It only requires that the bond shared by both parties is effectively destroyed. If this spell is performed with the right reasons and genuine intentions, it can also help to heal the pain of a heartbreak. This spell is best performed on a star-filled night in a lonely environment

Items that are needed are

- Blank parchment/ blank piece of paper
- Red ink
- Sharp scissors

How to cast the successful divorce spell

You require the right mindset to carry on with the spell. Analyze your situations and find out the reasons you want the divorce. Think about the situations that have prompted the divorce. Observe the feelings of sadness and grief which you feel and make a conscious effort to let go of it.

With your red ink pen, write "I release (Your partner's name) from my soul" on a paper. Let this be written nine different times in horizontal and vertical patterns. Start each of the sentences on a new line and write it in separately the gaps properly. When your intention is clearly written down on the paper and shut your eyes and focus your mind on the intentions you have clearly written on your paper. Cut the paper containing your intentions into smaller pieces using your pair of scissors. Bury the shredded paper under an old tree.

SPELLS FOR LOW SELF-ESTEEM

Low self- esteem is not the ideal behavioral trait for anyone because it affects the way the individual perceives the world and how they live with others. The implications of low self- esteem are usually very grave and are not advisable for anyone to possess. Anyone who lacks self- esteem is not living the right kind of life. Such a person would not realize what it takes to respect and admire themselves. This spell helps individuals learn to appreciate, love and respect themselves the more. it eradicates self -doubt and self- loathe. It gives you the energy to create the permission you need to love yourself and admire everything about yourself.

Items that are needed are
- Rose quartz
- Amethyst
- Rhodonite
- Citrine

How to cast the spell

Find a suitable position and make yourself feel comfortable. There are no rules for this. If you want to stay indoors, it is acceptable but if you are more comfortable staying outdoor, let it be.
Close your eyes and breathe slowly. Enjoy the beauty of your own breathe and relax with the thoughts of hearing yourself breathe. Let it be an activity that would course your entire being.

Find a place that suits your being settle comfortably into this newfound place you have located. Now, you can envision a walled place and everywhere seems warm and beautiful.

As you approached the walled garden, you will observe that the gate to the garden is locked but your name is inscribed on the gates of the garden. You will also notice that the place is your sacred garden and it is meant for only you.

Now, you will feel the key to the walled garden is in your pocket, put it into the lock. The gates have given way for entrance and the place is extremely beautiful. It is a perfect description of everything you have ever imagined and thought of.

Close the gate behind you and keep the keys safely in your possession and proceed to walk down the steps just beyond the gates of the garden. This new place you have arrived is the direct opposite of the walled garden. This place is dark, and the light is not enough to give the required illumination. You may have to walk with ease to prevent encountering a disaster because you can barely see the environment around you. As you step down into the well- decorated garden, you will notice a huge difference and the awful smell behind you.

 At this point, you can now explore the beauty of the garden and relish its beauty. A place you never thought you could have access to. You will realize you have the power to live within the beauty of the garden but to do that, you will have to do away with the dark areas and embrace the beauty of the garden.

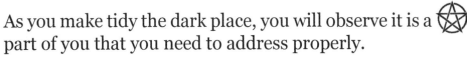

As you make tidy the dark place, you will observe it is a part of you that you need to address properly.

You also decide to clean up the beautiful garden. By so doing, you will find a bench in the garden and you may sit on it. Sitting on the bench will realize the bench is magical and has some sorts of healing magical powers. The healing light from the bench crawls into your being and completely removes every darkness and dark patch around your life.

You are entitled to sit there for as long as you want to and learn the lessons you need to learn from. Once the healing session is over, the healing light leaves you and the lessons are kept with you. From the lessons, you are learning to be better.

Now, you can walk freely around the garden to appreciate everything that you have lost and revel in the beauty of the garden. You also feel lighter and make your way back towards the gate of the garden.

As you are about to leave the garden, you take a swipe at the garden one last time and realize that all of the beauty contained in the garden can be all of yours. You also come to the realization that as long as it is contained on the outside, it can also be inside of you.

You can now return to your body and reflect on the lessons you have learnt. You are now equipped with the right knowledge of everything you ought to be and how you can be a better person who would learn to appreciate everything that concerns you the more. Now, you have completed the process, you have an opportunity to be a better person and also the ability to plan the kind of future you desire.

When you are ready to face the future head-on, open your eyes and come back to your physical surroundings and go back to your daily life.

SELF-EMPOWERMENT SPELL

This spell is most suitable for individuals who are always battling with poor self- esteem. For such indi- viduals, the spell can be performed every day.

Items you will need are

- A red-colored candle
- Matches
- Orange or lemon oil
- Yarrow herbs
- Self- esteem crystals
- Mantra

How to cast the spell

- The first step is to anoint the candle with some quantity of oil and then sprinkle some quantity of yarrow herb on it.
- Put on the candle
- Pay attention to the flame and come to the belief that it is actually raising your energy
- Pass the crystal through the flame whilst chanting the mantra

Let this be done as long as the candle is still burning fiercely and as long as the practitioner can. It can also be performed every day.

Whenever you feel your self-esteem is low ensured to visualize yourself carrying out the spell and then chant your mantra internally.

ACCEPTANCE SPELL

- One white candle
- One candle holder
- Matches/ lighter
- A piece of Paper
- A pan

How to cast the spell

The first step is to cast a circle

- On a piece of paper, write everything you find difficult to accept about yourself. Note the changes you want to make and how you haven't affected the desired changes
- With your matches/ lighter, put on the candle
- Pay attention to the flame from the candle
- Envision yourself letting go of every form of the negative attitude you are no longer comfortable. Imagine that all the doors are gradually opening up for you and accept the inner peace that you feel.
- Imagine yourself in a situation where you are experiencing the right kind of peace you desire
- Look at the flames from the fire as it moves around graciously
- Let go of the circle but allow the candle to burn out gradually. Ensure that you watch the candle as it turns out for security-based reasons to avoid taking chances and for safety reasons.
- When the candle is burned out and the wax has become cold, keep the wax somewhere safe; prefe-

rably in your bag or any container that possesses some space.

WAXING MOON MONEY SPELL:

The waxing moon is argued to occur in the first half of a lunar month. That is, it is a period where the moon is extremely bright, and its light produces a sufficient amount of light. The waxing moon is a period of time when it is easier to reach for wealth, prosperity and every other desire that the heart holds. At this instance, it is possible to get whatever thing the heart yearns for.

Items that are needed are

- A darker shade of brown candle. Brown is significant for its potency of attracting wealth and prosperity
- Aromatic spices
- Gold coin

How to cast the spell

- You need to wait for the waxing moon to perform this spell. For beginners who have never tried out this spell, it is better to consult people who are more experienced to guide you. If you make a mistake in identifying the waxing moon and perform this spell at the wrong time, there are bound to be consequences.
- Go to a quiet room that is only graced by the

presence of moonlight. Gather everything you require for the spell together and put on the candle. Pay attention to the flames from the candle.

• Now, you have to take in thirty deep breaths while envisioning yourself surrounded by the wealth and prosperity you desire.

• Place the gold coin between your palms together with some aromatic spices. Rub your palms together and inhale the fragrance from in between your palms.

Chant these words three times:

"MONEY FLOW, MONEY GROW, MONEY GLOW BLOW OUT THE CANDLE"

Carefully place the gold coin in your wallet. Whenever you want to go out ensure the gold coin is secure in your wallet. The results will be evident in a couple of weeks.

WAXING MOON BANISHING SPELL:

This spell is essential for eliminating unwanted energies and forces from a particular environment. This spell is usually performed when the individual is a peaceful state of mind and is not angry. There may be consequences to casting this kind of spell, so it is important for the practitioner to understand the exact period of the waxing moon.

Things you will need are:

- Apple cider vinegar
- Herbs such as rosemary, mint, and thyme
- Garlic cloves
- A glass

How the spell is casted

- Ensure the waxing moon is already out
- Go to a quiet place and put all the supplies that would be needed for the spell.
- Put the dried herbs (Rosemary, thyme, and mint) inside a jar and pour some quantity of apple cider vinegar over it.
- Close the jar properly and shake the contents together. With your eyes closed, pay attention to the energy you want to eliminate
- Envision the energy leaving you and do not accept the presence of any contrary force. Endeavor to maintain a calm physical demeanor all through the period and do not accept any negative emotion. Accept that the tightly closed jar is charged

- Keep the jar in a dark place safe for a period of about four to six weeks. After the period, sprinkle the contents of the jar outside your home and get rid of unwanted forces and enemies.

This was

WICCA ALTAR FOR BEGINNERS

the First book in Wicca Altar and Tools Series.
Please be sure to check out the other 2 books from the
same series.

WICCA TOOLS FOR BEGINNERS

WICCA SYMBOLS FOR BEGINNERS

Please consider leaving a great
5-Star review for this book

CPSIA information can be obtained
at www.ICGtesting.com
Printed in the USA
BVHW031159191120
593719BV00001B/26